A Special Gift

~

_____

A GIFT FOR:

_____

FROM:

_____

DATE:

A LASTING HERITAGE
FOR YOUR CHILDREN

~

A FATHER'S

Legacy

YOUR
LIFE STORY
IN YOUR OWN
WORDS

~

GIFT BOOKS
from Hallmark

BOK 4030

COUNTRYMAN

Contents

Introduction

"What grade did you get in high school English, Dad?"
"What did you do on your first date?" Sound familiar?
Your son or daughter has probably asked these questions
and many more. Why? Curiosity partly, but mostly because
they care—about you. They want to know what you did
when you were growing up because they want to know you.

That is the purpose of this book, which is a book about
you—your family history, your childhood memories,
humorous incidents, and meaningful traditions from your
life. It is a personal biography just waiting to be written.
Yes, there are planes to catch, meetings to attend, grass to
mow, and the car to wash, but those are not a legacy you
can pass on to your child. This book is.

Presented in a twelve-month format, this journal provides
an array of questions your son or daughter might ask with
space for your answers. Questions like, "Describe the most

fun you ever had on a Fourth of July." Or "When you went to a ball game as a boy, what kind of food did you eat?" Or "What is the nicest thing you ever did for your mother and father?"

These questions will help you write down the special memories, thoughts, and ideas you want to share with your children. You may choose to complete the journal in a few days, a few weeks, or throughout the course of the year. When you have filled in all of the pages you will have a loving memoir—a spiritual legacy—to pass on to your children. They will cherish this book about you for a lifetime.

This book is for fathers of all ages, because it is never too early or too late to share your life with those you love. May *A Father's Legacy* draw you closer to your children as you share this memoir of your life . . . straight from your heart to theirs.

Personal Portrait

YOUR FULL GIVEN NAME

YOUR DATE OF BIRTH

YOUR PLACE OF BIRTH

YOUR MOTHER'S FULL NAME

THE PLACE AND DATE OF HER BIRTH

YOUR FATHER'S FULL NAME

THE PLACE AND DATE OF HIS BIRTH

THE NAMES OF YOUR PATERNAL GRANDPARENTS

THE PLACES AND DATES OF THEIR BIRTHS

THE NAMES OF YOUR MATERNAL GRANDPARENTS

THE PLACES AND DATES OF THEIR BIRTHS

THE NAMES OF YOUR SIBLINGS

THE PLACES AND DATES OF THEIR BIRTHS

THE DATE AND PLACE OF YOUR MARRIAGE

THE FULL GIVEN NAME OF YOUR WIFE

THE NAMES AND BIRTH DATES OF YOUR CHILDREN

What is your favorite

SPORT

BOOK

LEISURE ACTIVITY

DESSERT

AUTHOR

BIBLE VERSE

HYMN OR SONG

VACATION SPOT

TYPE OF FOOD

SPORTS TEAM

January

Our stories are

inextricably interwoven.

What you do

is part of my story;

what I do is part of yours.

DANIEL TAYLOR

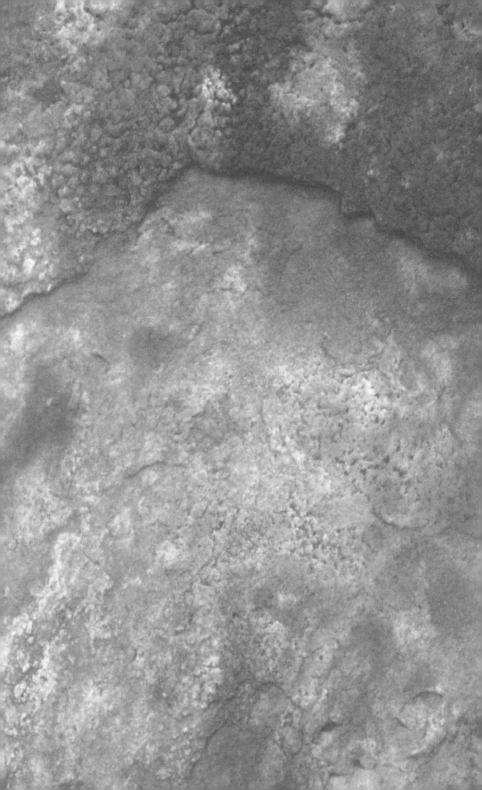

WHAT DID YOU ENJOY DOING MOST AS A CHILD? DID YOU PREFER DOING IT ALONE OR WITH SOMEONE ELSE?

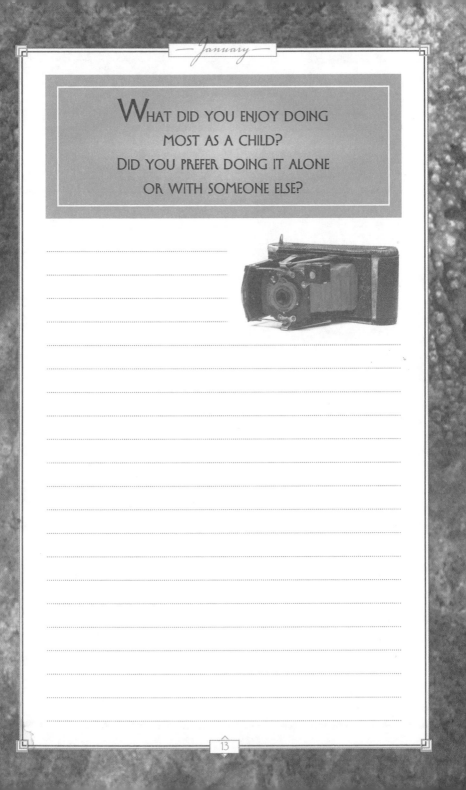

WHO GAVE YOU YOUR NAME AND WHY?
DID YOU HAVE A NICKNAME?
HOW DID YOU GET IT?

DESCRIBE YOUR CHILDHOOD HOME. WHAT WAS YOUR FAVORITE ROOM?

WERE YOU BAPTIZED OR
DEDICATED AS AN INFANT?
IF SO, WHERE AND BY WHOM?

Did you attend church as a young boy? What are your earliest memories of church?

WHERE DID YOUR FATHER GO TO WORK EVERY DAY AND WHAT DID HE DO? DID HIS WORK INTEREST YOU?

DID YOUR MOTHER HAVE A JOB OR DID SHE WORK AT HOME?

What was your favorite sport or outdoor activity? Why was this your favorite?

DID YOU PRAY AS A YOUNG BOY?
IF SO, CAN YOU REMEMBER A SPECIFIC PRAYER?
WHO TAUGHT YOU TO PRAY?

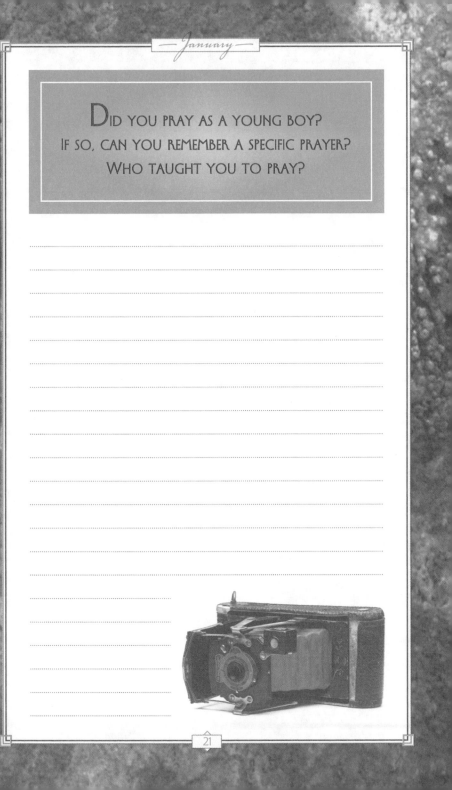

WHERE WAS YOUR CHILDHOOD HOME LOCATED? DID YOU ENJOY LIVING THERE?

Describe your grandparents. What did you enjoy most about them?

CAN YOU REMEMBER BEING AFRAID AS A BOY?
WHAT WAS YOUR GREATEST FEAR?
HOW DID YOU DEAL WITH IT?

RECALL FOR ME FIVE
OF THE MOST IMPORTANT LESSONS
YOU HAVE LEARNED IN LIFE.

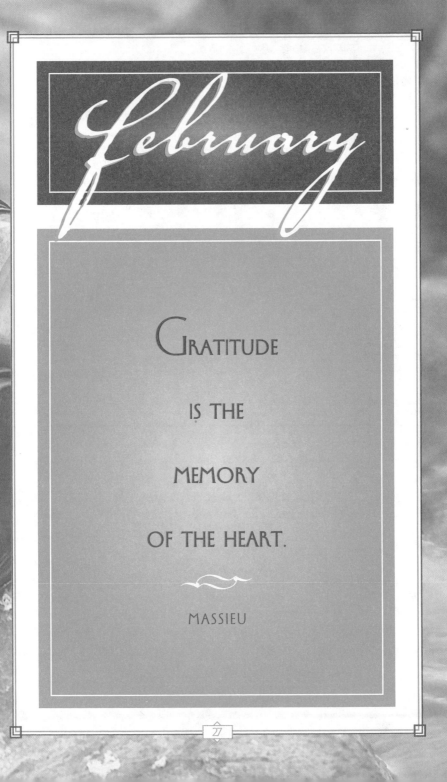

February

GRATITUDE

IS THE

MEMORY

OF THE HEART.

MASSIEU

Did the pastor or a visiting missionary ever eat dinner at your house? Did they have an impact on your life?

Did you ever feel that God had a special calling on your life?

Describe the most memorable
Valentine you ever received.
Who sent it to you?

How far did you have to travel to attend elementary, junior high, and high school, and how did you get there?

WHO GAVE YOU YOUR FIRST BIBLE
AND HOW OLD WHERE YOU
WHEN YOU RECEIVED IT.
HOW DID IT INFLUENCE YOUR LIFE?

—february—

WHEN DID YOU BECOME A CHRISTIAN? HOW DID YOUR LIFE CHANGE?

DID YOU GO TO BALL GAMES AS A BOY? WHAT KIND OF FOOD DID YOU EAT?

WHEN YOU WERE GROWING UP,
DID YOU HAVE ANY ANIMALS?
WHAT WERE THEIR NAMES?
WAS IT IMPORTANT TO YOU TO HAVE A PET?

TELL ME ABOUT YOUR MOTHER'S COOKING.
CAN YOU RECALL YOUR FAVORITE MEAL?
WHAT MADE IT YOUR FAVORITE?

Did you ever get into fights
with others kids?
Did you ever start a fight?
Or stop one?

WHAT CHORES DID YOU HAVE TO
DO WHEN YOU WERE GROWING UP?
DID YOU GET AN ALLOWANCE?
HOW MUCH WAS IT?

WHO GAVE YOU YOUR FIRST JOB?
WHAT KIND OF JOB WAS IT?
HOW MUCH MONEY DID YOU MAKE?

February

Share your idea of what makes a good friend.

March

W<small>E</small> HAVE

ONE LIFE TO LIVE—

AND ONE CHANCE

TO LIVE IT IN THE

RICHEST WAY POSSIBLE.

JUDITH THURMAN

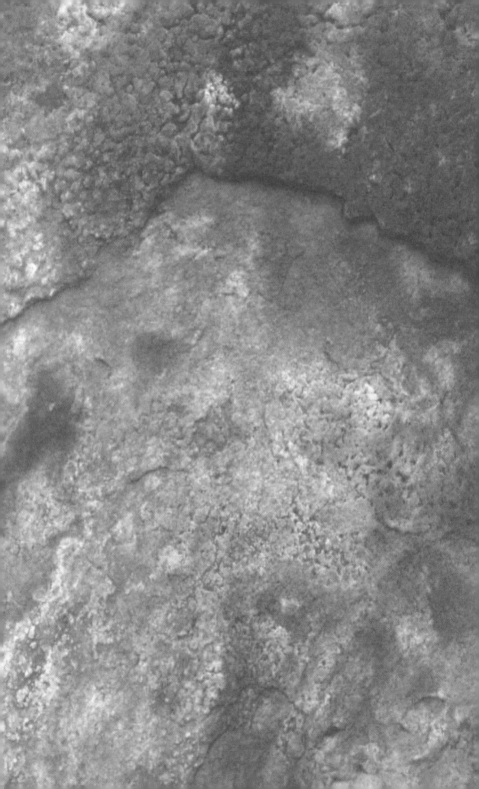

Do you remember your
first communion?
What influence did it have
on you and your family?

DESCRIBE YOUR FAVORITE PASTIME OR HOBBY AS A CHILD.

WHAT MISCHIEVOUS PRANK DID YOU PULL ON SOMEONE? HOW DID IT AFFECT YOU?

DID YOU HAVE A TELEVISION WHEN YOU WERE GROWING UP? WHAT WAS YOUR FAVORITE PROGRAM? WHY?

WHAT WERE SOME CRAZY FADS FROM YOUR SCHOOL DAYS? DID YOU PARTICIPATE IN THEM? WHY OR WHY NOT?

Who was your favorite teacher?
How did that teacher
influence your life?

Did you ever have a special
hideaway or clubhouse?
Describe it for me.

IN HIGH SCHOOL, WHAT EXTRACURRICULAR
ACTIVITIES DID YOU ENJOY MOST?
WHY DID YOU CHOOSE THOSE ACTIVITIES?

What is the nicest thing you ever did for your mother and father?

Did you admire a famous person? What made that person admirable?

When did you have your first date? Tell me about it.

WHAT DO YOU REMEMBER ABOUT YOUR FIRST KISS?

Share some of
your insights for working
well with others.

April

It is in the shelter

of each other

that the people live.

~

IRISH PROVERB

DID YOU ENJOY READING AS A BOY? WHAT WERE SOME OF THE MOST MEMORABLE BOOKS YOU READ?

WHAT WERE YOUR FAMILY FINANCES LIKE WHEN YOU WERE GROWING UP? HOW DID THAT AFFECT YOU?

W AS THERE A SPECIAL PERSON WHO
HELPED YOU IN YOUR CHRISTIAN WALK?
SHARE SOMETHING ABOUT THAT PERSON.

WHEN DID YOU FIRST LEARN ABOUT SEX?
WOULD YOU RECOMMEND THE SAME
FOR YOUNG PEOPLE TODAY?
WHY OR WHY NOT?

As a teenager did you rebel
or do things your parents
wouldn't have approved of?
How do you feel about that now?

LIST THREE THINGS YOU WISH YOU
HAD DONE DURING YOUR JUNIOR HIGH
AND HIGH SCHOOL YEARS, BUT DIDN'T.

—*April*—

What did your family like to do on weekends? Describe one particularly memorable one.

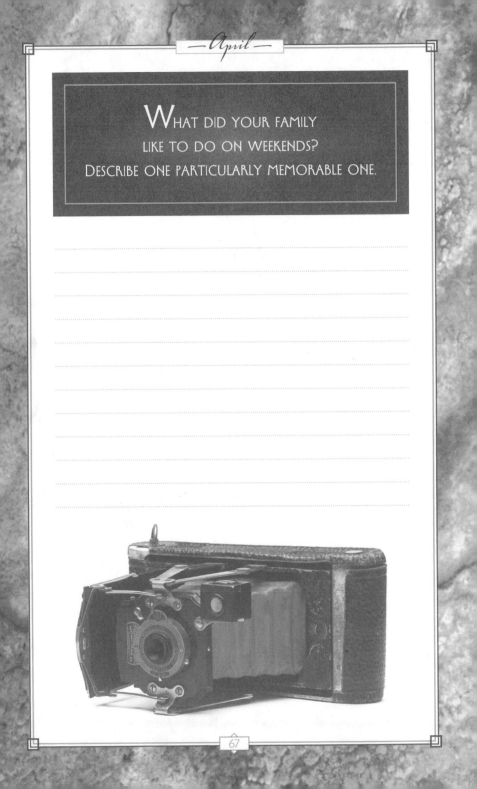

67

DURING CHILDHOOD, WHO WAS YOUR BEST FRIEND? SHARE SOME OF YOUR FONDEST MEMORIES OF FUN TIMES TOGETHER.

DID YOU EVER KEEP A SCRAPBOOK
OF PHOTOS, AUTOGRAPHS, OR
MEMORIES OF SPECIAL OCCASIONS?
DESCRIBE WHAT THIS MEANT TO YOU.

—April—

What is your favorite memory of your mother? Why is it so special to you?

WHAT IMAGE OF YOUR FATHER IS THE MOST STRIKING IN YOUR MEMORY? WHY THAT IMAGE?

LIST ONE SPECIAL MEMORY
ABOUT EACH OF YOUR
BROTHERS AND SISTERS.

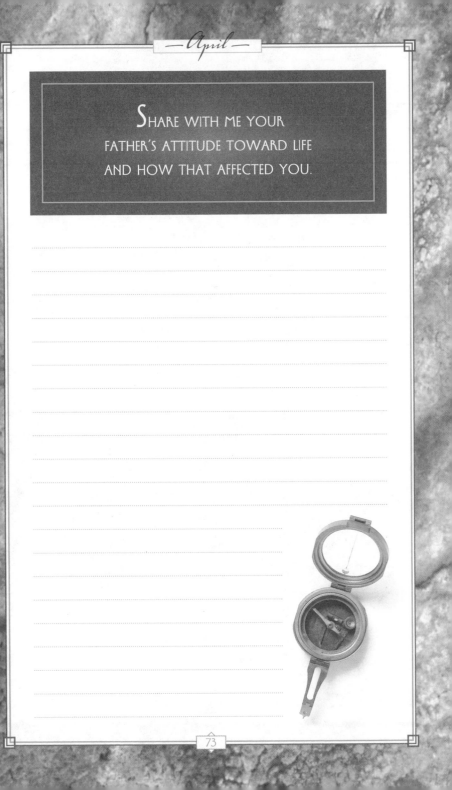

SHARE WITH ME YOUR
FATHER'S ATTITUDE TOWARD LIFE
AND HOW THAT AFFECTED YOU.

May

WHO,

BEING LOVED,

IS POOR?

OSCAR WILDE

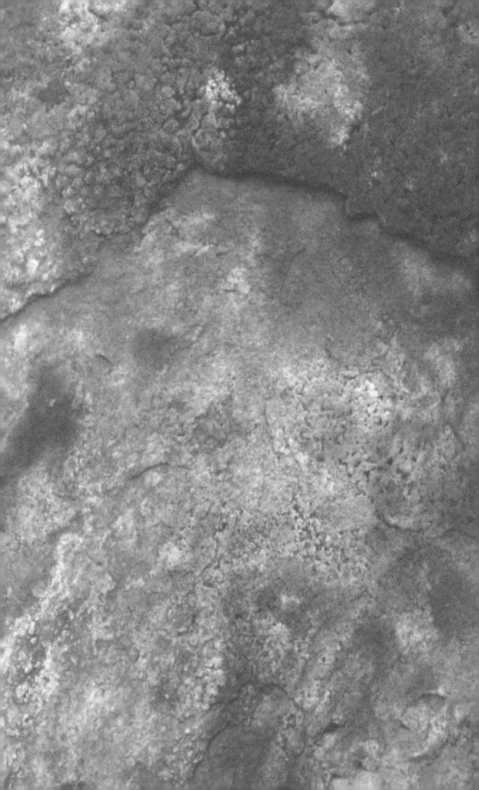

IF YOU WERE TO FIND AN OLD TOY BOX IN YOUR ATTIC, WHAT TOYS WOULD YOU REMEMBER MOST FONDLY? WHY?

How old were you when you understood that God loves you? How did that affect your life?

Describe a time in your life when you feel God led you in an unusual way.

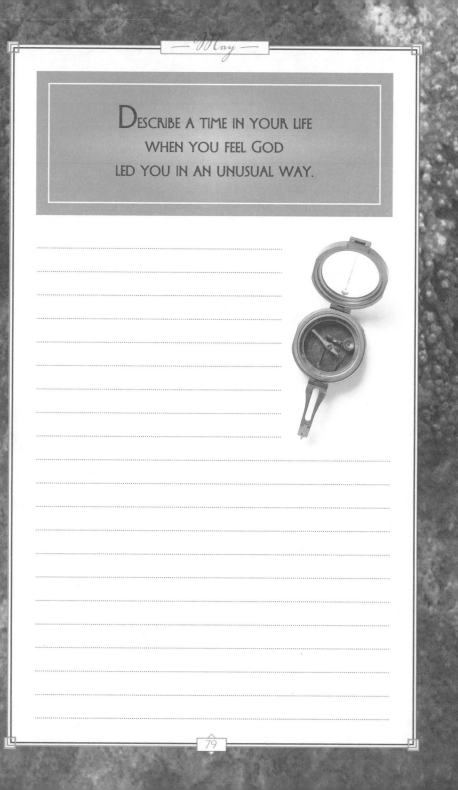

What kind of car did your family drive? Were you proud of it or embarrassed by it? Why?

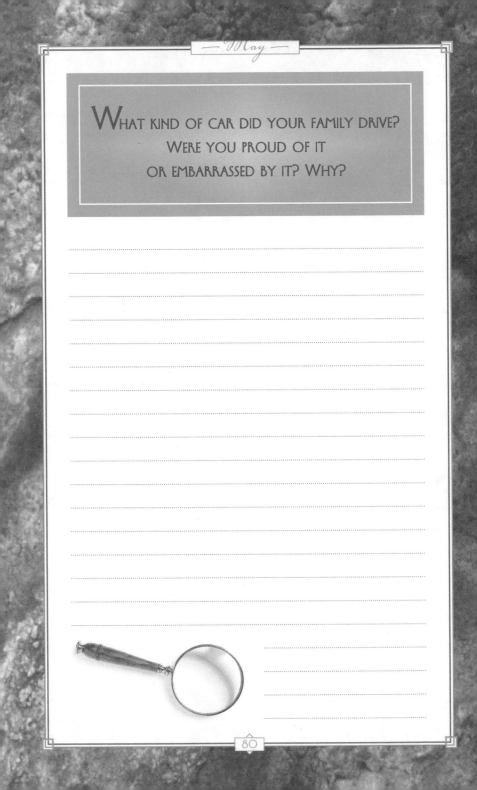

DID YOU EVER GO TO A DANCE? TELL ME ABOUT IT.

How often did your family go to church? What pastor or Sunday school teacher do you remember most? How did that person influence you?

DID YOUR FAMILY ATTEND FAMILY REUNIONS? WHAT ACTIVITIES DID EVERYONE ENJOY? TELL ME ABOUT YOUR FAVORITE COUSINS, AUNTS, OR UNCLES.

WHEN YOU WERE YOUNG,
DID YOU EVER GO TO A FUNERAL?
HOW DID THAT AFFECT YOU.

IF YOU HAD BROTHERS AND SISTERS, DID YOU FEEL YOUR PARENTS TREATED YOU ALL THE SAME? WHY OR WHY NOT? IF YOU WERE AN ONLY CHILD, DID YOU WISH FOR BROTHERS AND SISTERS? WHY?

Did your high school have college or career days? What field interested you most? What did you want to become when you grew up?

....
....
....
....
....
....
....
....
....
....
....
....
....
....
....
....
....
....
....

IF YOU WENT TO COLLEGE OR TO A CAREER TRAINING SCHOOL, WHERE DID YOU GO AND WHY?

WHERE DID YOU LIVE WHEN YOU WERE GOING
TO COLLEGE OR DEVELOPING A CAREER?
DESCRIBE AN UNFORGETTABLE EXPERIENCE
FROM THAT TIME IN YOUR LIFE.

SHARE SOME PRINCIPLES FROM SCRIPTURE
ON WHICH YOU HAVE
CHOSEN TO BUILD YOUR LIFE.

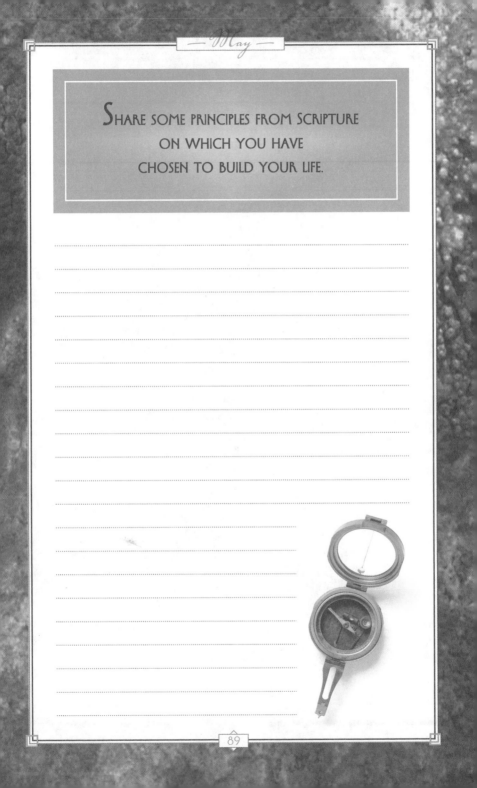

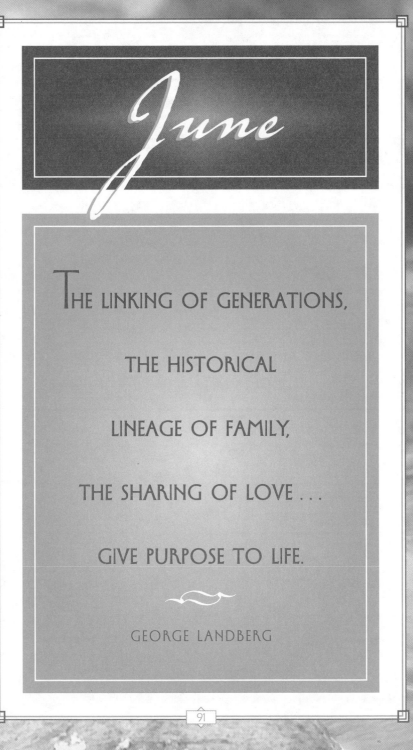

June

THE LINKING OF GENERATIONS,

THE HISTORICAL

LINEAGE OF FAMILY,

THE SHARING OF LOVE . . .

GIVE PURPOSE TO LIFE.

GEORGE LANDBERG

If you learned to play a musical instrument, tell me your memories of lessons, practice, and your music teacher. If not, what instrument did you want to play and why?

What were your youthful goals and ambitions for life? Which ones have you been able to fulfill?

How old were you when you met Mom? What attracted you to her?

WHEN DID YOU KNOW THAT MOM WAS
THE "ONE AND ONLY ONE" FOR YOU?
HOW DID YOU KNOW?

SHARE A MEMORY ABOUT THE
WAY YOU PROPOSED TO MOM.

Tell me about your wedding day. What happened? How did you feel? Were you nervous, scared, happy?

WHERE DID YOU GO ON YOUR HONEYMOON?
DESCRIBE AT LEAST ONE HUMOROUS
THING THAT HAPPENED TO YOU AND MOM.

Do you remember the first meals
mom cooked for you?
Do you dare comment on them?

Describe where you and Mom lived after you got married. What was the view like from the kitchen window?

WHEN DID YOU AND MOM
START TALKING ABOUT HAVING CHILDREN?
WHY DID YOU WANT CHILDREN—OR DID YOU?

IF YOU COULD GO ANYWHERE
IN THE WORLD ON A SECOND HONEYMOON,
WHERE WOULD YOU GO? WHY?

WHAT DO YOU LOVE BEST
ABOUT MOM NOW?

RECORD HERE YOUR IDEAS ON WHAT
IT TAKES FOR A HUSBAND AND WIFE
TO MAINTAIN A HEALTHY MARRIAGE.

July

Somehow, year after year, Dad managed to take us on vacations he couldn't afford to provide, in order to make memories that we couldn't afford to be without.

RICHARD EXLEY

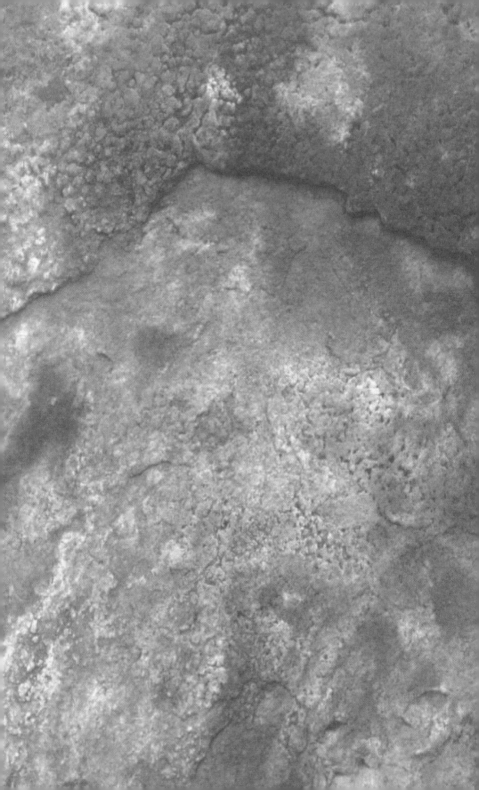

DESCRIBE THE MOST FUN YOU EVER HAD ON A FOURTH OF JULY.

TELL ME ABOUT YOUR FAMILY SUMMER
OUTINGS WHEN YOU WERE YOUNG.
DID YOU GO CAMPING? FISHING? SWIMMING?

DID YOU EVER TRAVEL ABROAD? HOW OLD WERE YOU AND WHERE DID YOU GO?

WHO IS THE MOST INTERESTING FOREIGNER
YOU HAVE EVER MET?
WHAT DID THIS PERSON HELP YOU
LEARN ABOUT HIS OR HER CULTURE?

IF YOU SERVED IN THE ARMED FORCES, DESCRIBE HOW YOUR TIME IN THE SERVICE AFFECTED YOUR LIFE. IF YOU DID NOT SERVE, HOW DID THIS AFFECT YOUR LIFE?

Have you ever believed so strongly in a cause that you marched in a rally or demonstrated in protest? What was the cause? Why was it important to you?

What is the gutsiest thing you ever did in your life? Why did you do it?

WHERE DO YOU STAND POLITICALLY?
DO YOU LEAN TOWARD THE LEFT OR THE RIGHT?
WHO, IF ANYONE, HAS MOST GREATLY INFLUENCED
YOUR CURRENT POLITICAL VIEWS?

Did a tragedy ever strike your family? If so, how did it affect you?

WHAT IS THE BEST MOVIE YOU'VE EVER SEEN?
IF YOU COULD PLAY ONE OF THE
CHARACTERS IN THE FILM,
WHOM WOULD YOU CHOOSE, AND WHY?

How would you finish this sentence?
"One thing my dad always said was..."

DID YOU EVER GO TO SUMMER CAMP?
CAMPING WITH THE BOY SCOUTS?
SHARE ONE UNFORGETTABLE MEMORY.

SHARE A FAVORITE POEM,
PASSAGE OF WRITING, OR SOME
QUOTES THAT HAVE BEEN ESPECIALLY
MEANINGFUL IN YOUR LIFE.

August

W HEN I COME HOME

FROM WORK AND SEE

THOSE LITTLE NOSES PRESSED

AGAINST THE WINDOW PANE,

THEN I KNOW I AM A SUCCESS.

PAUL FAULKNER

IS THERE ANY ONE BOOK OR AUTHOR WHO
HELPED YOU TO DEVELOP A PHILOSOPHY OF LIFE?
SHARE SOME OF THOSE INSIGHTS.

How have your ideas about God changed from when you were young?

WHAT KIND OF OUTDOOR
WORK DO YOU ENJOY? DISLIKE?

WHAT IS YOUR FAVORITE WAY TO SPEND A DAY OF LEISURE?

WHEN DID YOU LEARN HOW TO
RIDE A BIKE, OR TO WATER SKI,
SNOW SKI, ROLLER SKATE, OR SAIL?
SHARE YOUR MEMORIES OF THE EXPERIENCE.

DID YOU EVER MILK A COW OR SPEND TIME
ON A FARM OR IN THE COUNTRY?
TELL ME ABOUT IT.

WHAT PLACES IN THE WORLD
WOULD YOU STILL LIKE TO VISIT? WHY?

IS THERE ANY CHILDHOOD FEAR
THAT STILL HAUNTS YOU?
HOW DO YOU DEAL WITH THIS FEAR?

How do you enjoy helping people? Share about a time when you helped someone in need.

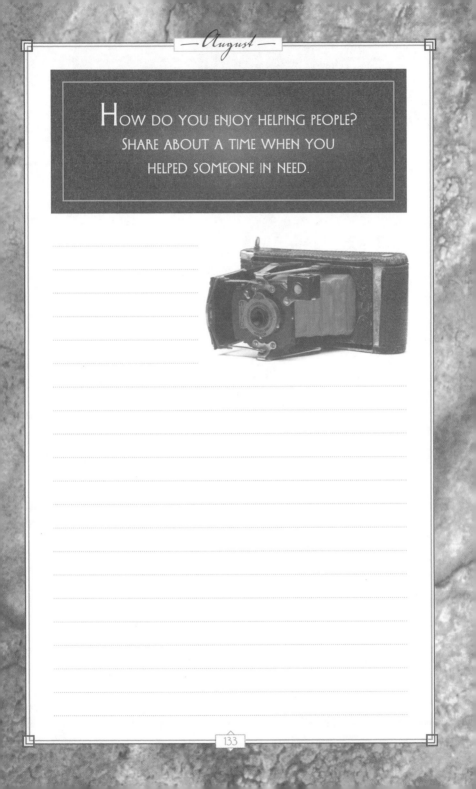

IF YOU COULD CARVE ONE MORE FACE ON MT. RUSHMORE, WHOSE FACE WOULD IT BE? WHY?

In what ways are you like
your mother? Like your father?

— August —

LOOKING BACK IN LIFE, WHAT ONE THING WOULD YOU HAVE DONE DIFFERENTLY? WHY?

Share some tips for a great vacation.

September

What lies behind us

and what lies before us

are tiny matters

compared to what

lies within us.

RALPH WALDO EMERSON

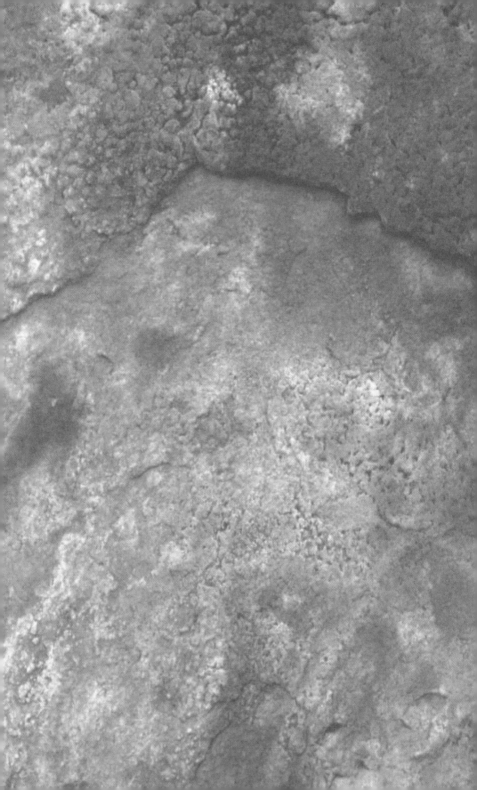

DID YOU LEARN MECHANICS OR
WOODWORKING AS A YOUNG PERSON?
HOW AND WHEN? WHAT WERE SOME OF
YOUR MOST MEMORABLE PROJECTS?

TELL ABOUT A SPECIAL OUTING
YOU TOOK WITH YOUR DAD.
WHAT MAKES THIS A
POIGNANT MEMORY FOR YOU?

As a young person did you volunteer for work in church, community, or social services? Tell me about it.

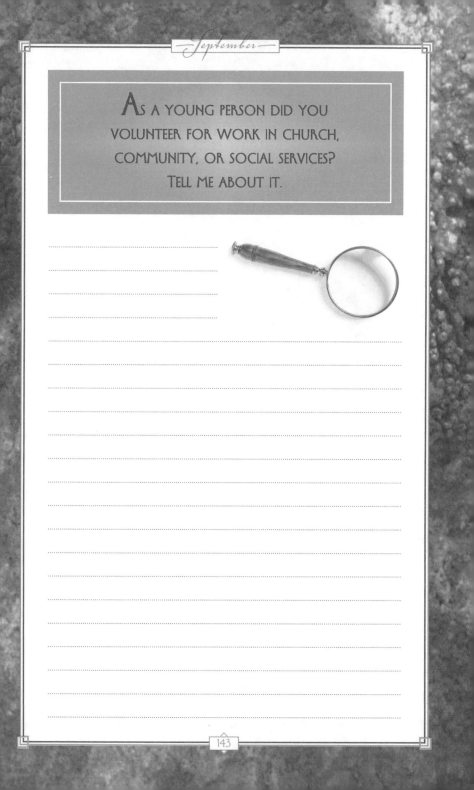

WHEN DID YOU MOVE AWAY FROM HOME? DESCRIBE WHERE YOU LIVED AND HOW YOU FELT ABOUT IT.

TELL ME ABOUT SOME OF YOUR CLOSEST FRIENDS
AFTER YOU AND MOM GOT MARRIED.
WHAT WERE SOME OF THE FUN THINGS
YOU WOULD DO TOGETHER?

WHAT ARE
YOUR SPIRITUAL STRENGTHS?

HOW WOULD YOU LIKE TO GROW SPIRITUALLY?

WHAT WOULD YOU STILL LIKE TO LEARN TO DO? WHY?

....

....

....

....

....

....

....

....

....

....

....

....

WHAT DID YOU ENJOY DOING WITH YOUR MOM? SHARE A SPECIAL TIME WITH HER.

How would you describe yourself: tender-hearted or tough-minded?

IF YOU WERE TO WRITE A BOOK ABOUT MOM,
HOW WOULD YOU TITLE THE BOOK?
THE FIRST FEW CHAPTERS?

How do you describe
"success"?

October

Life's journey is curcular,

it appears.

The years don't carry us

away from our father —

they return us to them.

~

MICHEL MARRIOTT

WHO ARE SOME OF THE BEST PUBLIC SPEAKERS YOU HAVE EVER HEARD? WHY DID THEY IMPRESS YOU?

IF YOU COULD HAVE TWO HOURS OF
CONVERSATION WITH ANYONE ON EARTH,
WHO WOULD THAT BE? WHY THAT PERSON?
WHAT WOULD YOU TALK ABOUT?

WHAT SPIRITUAL LEGACY WOULD YOU LIKE TO LEAVE FOR OTHERS? WHY IS THIS IMPORTANT TO YOU?

Share a hilarious travel experience.

WHAT BIBLE VERSE OR SCRIPTURE
PUZZLES YOU THE MOST?
WHICH BLESSES YOU THE MOST? WHY?

HAVE YOU EVER BEEN IN AN ACCIDENT, HAD SURGERY OR A LONG ILLNESS? HOW DID THIS AFFECT YOUR OUTLOOK ON LIFE?

Do you have a favorite sports team? Why is that one your favorite?

WHAT RESPONSIBILITIES DID YOUR PARENTS REQUIRE OF YOU AS A CHILD? HOW DID THIS AFFECT YOUR GROWTH AND DEVELOPMENT? HOW YOU RAISED YOUR CHILDREN?

WHAT IS THE MOST FRIGHTENING THING
THAT HAS EVER HAPPENED TO YOU?
HOW DID YOU HANDLE THE EXPERIENCE?

WHAT EVENTS IN LIFE HAVE STRENGTHENED
OR WEAKENED YOUR BELIEF IN PRAYER.

WHEN AND WHERE DID YOU BUY
YOUR FIRST HOUSE OR PIECE OF REAL ESTATE?
DESCRIBE THE SIGNIFICANCE THIS HELD FOR YOU.

WHAT IS THE STRANGEST THING YOU HAVE EVER SEEN?

Share some of your ideas on
how to develop and maintain
good physical health.

November

GOD CALLS

EACH GENERATION TO

PASS DOWN

SPIRITUAL TRUTH

TO THE NEXT.

DENNIS RAINEY

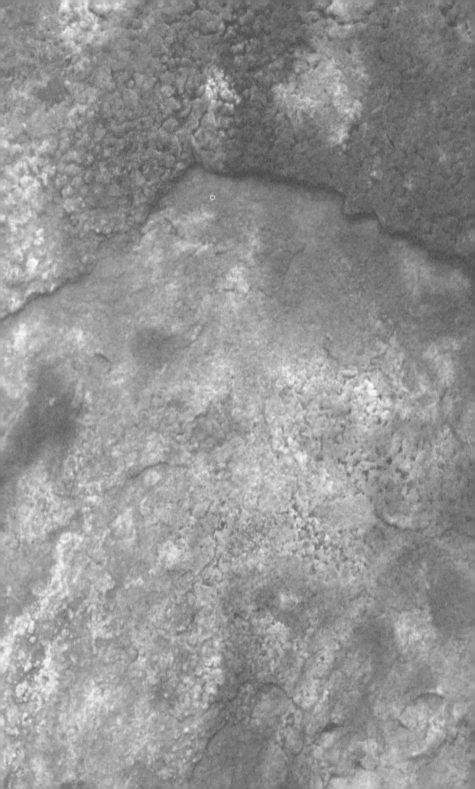

As a teenager, did you belong to a club or church youth group? Tell me about the individuals in the group who were most significant to you.

WHAT IS YOUR MOST TREASURED POSSESSION AND WHY?

WHAT BIBLE CHARACTER WOULD YOU MOST LIKE TO MEET? WHY?

WHAT TWO PEOPLE HAVE MADE
THE GREATEST SPIRITUAL IMPACT ON YOUR LIFE?
WHAT MADE THEM SO SIGNIFICANT TO YOU?

....

....

....

....

....

....

....

....

....

....

....

....

....

....

....

....

....

....

....

....

....

WHEN YOU WERE A NEW FATHER, WHAT WAS YOUR GREATEST FEAR? YOUR GREATEST JOY?

What is your most
vivid memory about my childhood?

WHAT WOULD YOU CHANGE ABOUT MY CHILDHOOD IF YOU COULD?

Describe a fond Thanksgiving memory.
What makes this special to you?

WHAT ARE SOME THINGS FROM YOUR CHILDHOOD THAT YOU ARE THANKFUL FOR?

WHAT CHILDHOOD MEMORY FIRST COMES
TO MIND WHEN YOU THINK ABOUT WINTER?
HOW DO YOU RESPOND TO THAT MEMORY?

DESCRIBE THE MOST INTERESTING PERSON
YOU EVER MET. WHAT WERE THE QUALITIES THAT
MADE THAT INDIVIDUAL SO OUTSTANDING?

WHAT FAMILY CUSTOMS OR TRADITIONS
WOULD YOU LIKE TO PASS ON TO
YOUR CHILDREN AND GRANDCHILDREN.
WHY ARE THEY IMPORTANT TO YOU?

TELL ME WHAT FOUR THINGS YOU WOULD NEVER LEAVE BEHIND ON A TRIP AND EXPLAIN WHY.

December

THOSE WHO LOVED YOU

AND WERE HELPED BY YOU

WILL REMEMBER YOU.

SO CARVE YOUR NAME ON

HEARTS AND NOT ON MARBLE.

C.H. SPURGEON

DESCRIBE SOME CHRISTMAS TRADITIONS
FROM YOUR CHILDHOOD AND TELL HOW
THEY HAVE INFLUENCED YOUR LIFE.

WERE YOU EVER IN A CHRISTMAS PROGRAM? HOW DID YOU RESPOND TO THE EXPERIENCE?

What is the best Christmas present you ever received? Why was that the best?

TELL ABOUT A MEMORABLE
CHRISTMAS VISIT WITH RELATIVES.

WHAT IS YOUR FAVORITE CHRISTMAS CAROL? WHY?

What would be the most wonderful gift you could receive? Why?

TELL ME ABOUT A TIME WHEN
GOD ANSWERED A SPECIFIC PRAYER FOR YOU.

WHAT WOULD YOU LIKE TO SEE HAPPEN
IN THE NEXT TEN YEARS IN YOUR LIFE?
IN THE WORLD?

As you look back in life, name three of
the most fantastic changes that have
taken place in the world.
How have these affected your life?

W HERE WOULD YOU STILL LIKE TO GO
AND WHAT WOULD YOU LIKE TO DO
ONCE YOU GOT THERE?

WHAT IS YOUR FAVORITE WAY TO SPEND A RAINY DAY?

WHAT WORD BEST DESCRIBES YOUR LIFE? EXPLAIN WHY.

What advice about life do you want others to remember?